NATIONAL
GEOGRAPHIC

# Water

## George Huxley

# Water comes in different forms.
It can be a liquid, a solid, or a gas.

Liquid

Solid

**Gas**

3

When water is a liquid, it moves freely. It takes the shape of its container. The water in a glass is a liquid.

Where else can you find water as a liquid?

The water in a river is a liquid.
The water in a river moves freely.
It takes the shape of the riverbed.

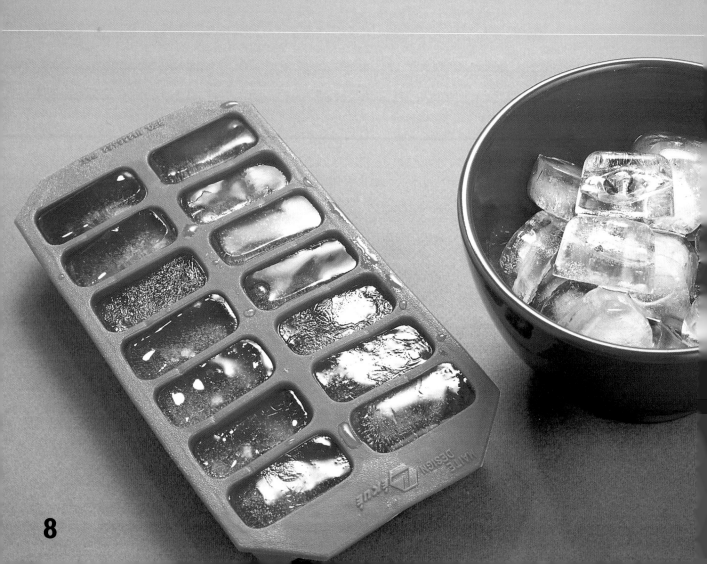

When water is a solid, it is hard.
It keeps its shape.
Ice cubes are solids.

Where else can you find water as a solid?

An iceberg is a solid.
The water in an iceberg is hard.
It keeps its chunky shape.

12

When water is a gas, it spreads through the air.
The steam that rises from a kettle of boiling water is a gas.

Where else can you find water as a gas?

The steam that rises from a hot spring is a gas. As the steam rises, it spreads through the air.

# Picture Glossary

## Liquid

## Solid

## Gas